Breathe Easy

Young People's Guide to
Asthma

SECOND EDITION

written by
Jonathan H. Weiss, Ph.D.

illustrated by
Michael Chesworth

MAGINATION PRESS • WASHINGTON, DC

Published by
MAGINATION PRESS
An Educational Publishing Foundation Book
American Psychological Association
750 First Street, NE
Washington, DC 20002

For more information about our books, including a complete catalog,
please write to us, call 1-800-374-2721,
or visit our website at www.maginationpress.com.

Library of Congress Cataloging-in-Publication Data

Weiss, Jonathan H.
Breathe easy : young people's guide to asthma / Jonathan H. Weiss ;
illustrated by Michael Chesworth.— 2nd ed.
p. cm.
Summary: Teaches control of frequency and severity of asthma attacks
through awareness of asthma triggers, relaxation exercises, and medications.
Contains resources and a parent guide.
ISBN 1-55798-956-7 (hc : alk. paper) — ISBN 1-55798-957-5 (pbk : alk. paper)
1. Asthma in children—Juvenile literature. [1. Asthma. 2. Diseases.]
I. Chesworth, Michael, ill. II. Title.
RJ436.A8 W45 2002
618.92'238—dc21

2002015082

Manufactured in the United States of America
10 9 8 7 6 5 4 3 2 1

Contents

Preface

Despite a decade in which the mechanisms and treatment of asthma have been greatly clarified, the number of asthma sufferers in the United States is growing. Today, that number is more than 17 million, up from 6.7 million in 1980. Too often asthma is not recognized in its early stages, when prompt intervention could prevent hospitalizations and emergency room visits. Improper use of medications, mistaken ideas, and inadequate knowledge also contribute to the problem. The resulting costs include millions of physician visits, school days lost, and dollars spent on medications and treatments.

But the picture is not all grim. New medications have been developed to help both prevent and control symptoms. Our understanding of the mechanisms of asthma has increased. And we have learned that the most effective treatment occurs when there is a partnership between the patient, family, and physicians.

In this updated and expanded edition of the best-selling *Breathe Easy*, Dr. Jonathan Weiss presents the how, when, why, where, and what of asthma. His message is clear: You can control your asthma. With the help of illustrations, he describes early warning signs, relaxation exercises, allergy triggers, and what to do if an asthma attack occurs. In short, the patient and family are part of the asthma management team, providing intervention even before a physician can.

I recommend that both parent and child read this book together. The understanding that will be gained will lead to a more secure outlook concerning asthma—and to a better quality of life.

IRWIN RAPPAPORT, M.D.
Clinical Professor of Pediatrics
Weill Medical College of Cornell University
Former Director, Division of Allergy & Immunology
New York Presbyterian Hospital

Introduction

"Tell them they can get better! Be upbeat."

This is the advice of a 13-year-old boy, one of my patients, to young people his age who are learning to control their asthma. He's right. People with asthma can get better and lead healthy and productive lives. Many people with asthma, such as Olympic runner Jackie Joyner Kersee, Pittsburgh Steelers' running back Jerome Bettis, actor Joe Pesci, and former President of the United States Theodore Roosevelt, have achieved great things. There are plenty of reasons to be upbeat.

If you're reading this book, you probably have asthma and want to do something to make it better. At the same time, you're probably busy with school and other activities, and don't want to spend a lot of time thinking about asthma. Great! Asthma is only a small part of your life, and controlling it should take up only a small part of your time and energy.

The techniques described in this book are designed to help you do just that. Some of them you may already know. Others will be new to you. They are simple and can be learned in just a few minutes a day over a period of a few weeks.

Share this book with members of your family, so that they can learn the techniques too and help you practice

them. At the same time, they will learn more about your asthma and how it makes you feel.

After you have practiced these techniques—and remember, it does take practice to master something—you will be able to spot and avoid many of the things that bring on, or trigger, your symptoms. You will be better at knowing how to tell if an attack is starting, and how to keep it from getting worse. Asthma will stop being so mysterious or frightening. And controlling it will become a lot easier for you and your family.

You'll find yourself spending less time being sidelined by attacks and more time doing the things you want to do. You will be more self-confident as you overcome many of the problems that living with asthma may now be causing you and your family— problems such as a million *do*'s and *don't*'s, feeling different or embarrassed because you have asthma and take medicine for it, being afraid to play sports because doing so might bring on an attack, panicking when you get an attack, and being afraid to travel away from home.

Are you ready to find out more—and worry less— about your asthma? Then let's begin!

What Is Asthma? 1

Asthma is a lung disorder that causes people to have trouble breathing. Approximately 17 million people in the United States live with asthma, and more than 4.3 million of them are children under the age of 18. The number of people with asthma is growing. Although doctors and scientists are learning more about asthma, nobody knows exactly why this is.

An increase in air pollution may be one reason why more people are developing asthma. Pollution from cars and industrial plants can create *toxins* (harmful substances) that irritate air passages in the lungs, and people may live in areas where it's especially hard to control being around such things.

There is also indoor air pollution, which is caused by such things as draperies, carpets, construction materials, and pets. People may be spending more time indoors (watching TV, using the computer, doing homework) and being exposed to things in their houses that trigger asthma.

Recently, researchers have discovered that children who don't go to nursery school get asthma more often than children who do. This may be because their bodies haven't had the chance to learn to handle substances that can trigger asthma. They haven't been around the things that can trigger asthma as much as kids in nursery school or day care, so their bodies haven't learned to adjust to those things in better ways. In a sense, they've been too clean!

We don't know exactly what causes asthma, although doctors are getting closer to the answers. We do know, however, that asthma isn't something that you catch like a cold or the flu. We also know that it doesn't come from emotional problems. Kids with asthma are like other kids in every way, except that they get asthma attacks. They are as brainy, goofy, talented, good looking, outrageous, ambitious, and friendly as any other group of kids. And we know that asthma tends to runs in families. If you have asthma, there's a good chance that someone else in your family does, too.

What seems to be inherited is an alarm system in your body that works overtime. Your body has a number of alarms. They tell you when something is

wrong and alert you to do something about it. For example, when you touch something hot, you feel pain, which tells you to pull your hand away. When you are in the path of danger, fear gets you to move out of its way. These alarms protect you. You'd be in trouble if they stopped working. However, you can also have trouble if your alarms work more than they need to. For example, some people feel pain when nothing is wrong, and others feel frightened by things that aren't really dangerous.

The alarm system that may cause asthma by working overtime is called the *immune system*. Its job is to protect you against harmful germs and viruses that invade your body and cause illnesses such as the flu or food poisoning. The immune system learns how to recognize those invaders and destroy them.

However, if the immune system works overtime— maybe because it produces too much of the "ammunition" that destroys invaders, or because it hasn't learned to identify what is truly harmful—it can attack things that aren't dangerous, such as dust or foods or pollen from plants. When this happens, the part of the body in which the attack takes place can become red and swollen, or *inflamed*. That's called an *allergic reaction*. If the part of your body that becomes inflamed is your lungs, you can have an asthma attack.

How We Breathe

Before we describe how an asthma attack works, let's take a look at normal breathing.

Look at the picture on this page. This shows our breathing, or *respiratory system*. You'll notice that the lungs look like an upside-down tree. The "trunk" of the tree is called the *trachea*. At its top, the trachea connects to the nose and mouth, whose job it is to clean, warm, and moisten the air you breathe. At its lower end, the trachea connects to the two big branches of the tree, the *bronchi*. These connect to the lungs, where they divide into smaller and smaller branches, called *bronchioles*. (In fact, the system is often called the *bronchial tree*.)

The bronchioles end up in what look like the leaves of the tree, the *alveoli*, which are small air-

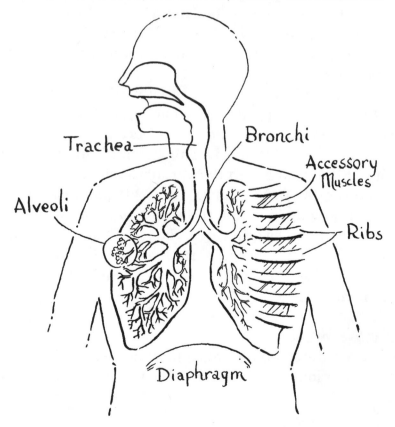

containing sacs. In the walls of the alveoli, blood comes to take oxygen from the air you breathe and carry it to the parts of your body that need it. The blood also drops off the used-up air called carbon dioxide in the alveoli so that you can breathe it out.

How do we get air to move in and out of the respiratory system? Look at the picture again. Below the lungs, find the *diaphragm*, which is shaped like an upside-down bowl. It's big and strong, and it's meant to be your main breathing muscle. When the diaphragm flattens down, it acts like a vacuum cleaner, sucking air into the bronchial tree and filling up the lungs. When it goes back to being shaped like an upside-down bowl, it pushes used-up air out of the lungs through the nose and mouth.

Now find the *accessory muscles* at the top of the ribs and chest. These muscles are smaller than the diaphragm and are meant to help when you need extra air, such as when you exercise or climb stairs. Many people with asthma breathe mainly with the accessory muscles rather than with the diaphragm. That is a mistake that with practice, and with the help of your family, you will learn not to make.

When you breathe the right way, with your diaphragm, you will get more air, more easily. During an attack of asthma, this can help you feel more comfortable.

Anatomy of an Asthma Attack

Now let's see what happens inside the body during an asthma attack. Look at the picture on page 12. One way to understand an asthma attack is to think

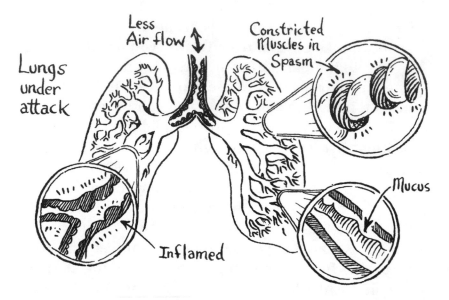

Lungs under attack

Less Air flow

Constricted Muscles in Spasm

Mucus

Inflamed

of the respiratory system as a network of highways on which air travels from the nose and mouth to the alveoli.

When the airways are normal, the highways are wide open and "traffic" moves smoothly and quickly. When you have an asthma attack, however, the highways get blocked and traffic has trouble moving in and out. Some of it gets trapped in the lungs, and you can't empty them. That's what keeps you from taking a nice, deep next breath.

Look at the picture again. Notice that parts of the lungs are swollen and inflamed during an asthma attack. Notice also that *mucus*, a liquid that keeps your lungs moist and smooth, has gotten thick and gummy and plugged up the airways. And notice that in other places, muscles around the airways have gone into spasm and tightened until the airways are squeezed almost shut. Everybody's lung muscles usually tighten when they are irritated by a whiff of smoke or some other toxin, but during an asthma attack the muscles seem to stay tight.

During an asthma attack your chest feels tight and you wheeze because the air you breathe is forced to pass through blocked, narrowed passages. Medicines called *bronchodilators* open—or dilate— the passages and make the tightness and wheezing go away.

However, doctors have discovered that even after your airways have relaxed and opened up again, they are still inflamed. The immune system continues to work overtime, so an attack can come back even more severely just when it seems to be over. An attack can sometimes last for days or weeks after the first symptoms seem to be over because the inflammation is still there. In order to really control your asthma, you have to do more than get rid of the tightness and wheezing. You also have to control the inflammation. Later in this book, you will learn about medicines that do that.

How an Attack Feels

Nobody knows better than you how an asthma attack feels. If the attack is mild, you may only need to slow down and make sure that you take your medicine the way your doctor told you to. You may cough or wheeze a little, but your breathing may not feel all that different.

If the attack is moderate, you may find yourself having to slow down and rest. Your chest may feel tight and tickly, and you may cough and wheeze.

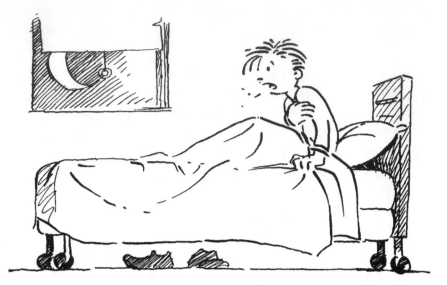

Trying to be active may make you feel even more out of breath, and you may have to wait for your medicine to work before you feel up to following your normal routine.

If the attack is more severe, you may find yourself exhausted from thinking about every breath you take. You may feel hungry for air and unable to take a deep breath, frustrated because activities that you usually do with ease leave you wheezing and gasping, and restless because you can't find a comfortable way to lie or sit that lets you breathe easily.

If the attack occurs in the middle of the night, you might feel more than just uncomfortable and frustrat-

Hint!

If you get night asthma, you might want to ask your parents to purchase an inexpensive intercom or monitor system. Put one station in your bedroom and the other in your parents' bedroom. If you have trouble in the middle of the night, you'll know that you can quickly call someone.

ed. Sitting up alone, unable to breathe when everybody else is asleep, you might be frightened and worried. You may even fear you will die. Later on in this book, we will talk about how people can frighten themselves by thinking scary thoughts, and how you can control your thoughts so that you feel less afraid.

Did you know that very few people actually die of asthma? The people who have the most trouble usually have not learned how to live with their asthma. By learning all you can about how to prevent attacks, and how to best handle them when they can't be avoided, you can take control of your asthma so that it won't control you.

You don't need to be afraid. You are learning how to take care of yourself. And you are not alone. Other people, like your family and your doctor, are there to help you stay safe and healthy. If you feel worried or afraid, share your feelings with them. When you are armed with knowledge and support from your doctor and your family, you'll be more confident and your fears will fade, perhaps disappearing altogether.

How Controlled Is Your Asthma?

In the past two weeks:
- Have you coughed, wheezed, or felt short of breath?
- Have you had chest tightness:
  —during the day?
  —at night causing you to wake up?
  —during or soon after exercise?

- Have you needed more quick-relief medicine than usual?
- Has your asthma kept you from doing anything you wanted to do?

In the past few months:
- Have you missed school because of asthma?
- Have you gone to the emergency room because of your asthma?

If you're like most kids who have asthma, you answered yes to at least one of these questions. This book can show you ways to minimize attacks and help you bring any problem areas you have under better control.

Are you ready to learn? Let's begin!

Asthma 2 Triggers

The first step in taking charge of your asthma is to find out what kinds of things trigger—or bring on—your attacks. The second step is to learn ways to control and avoid these triggers. You and your family can work together to help you control and avoid triggers that bring on your asthma.

Finding out what your triggers are isn't hard, and avoiding them doesn't mean that you will have to give up a lot of things that you like. Chances are, you already know some of your triggers. Even if you don't know how to avoid all of them, you probably already practice some control. For example, you may already stay away from cats, or your sport may be swimming instead of long-distance running. The more you know about your triggers and how to avoid them, the less likely you are to have attacks that seem to come out of nowhere, forcing you to cancel plans at the last minute or drop out in the middle of a group activity.

Finding Your Asthma Triggers

The following list of triggers has been put together from interviews with hundreds of kids who have asthma. Some of these triggers may bring on your asthma, and some may not. As you read through the list, pause after each trigger and try to recall any times when you experienced or were exposed to it. Try to remember if those were also times when your chest got tight or wheezy, right away or soon afterward. If so, put a check mark next to that trigger. If you clearly remember being exposed to or experiencing the trigger and *not* getting asthma, put a zero next to it. If you aren't sure, put a question mark next to the trigger.

__Exercise
__Overexertion (pushing yourself too hard or for too long)
__Getting upset (worried, angry, scared, sad)
__Getting excited (happy, eager, pleased)
__Laughing
__Coughing
__Sneezing
__Crying
__Choking (swallowing down the wrong pipe)
__Catching a cold
__Night time attacks (going to sleep clear and waking up wheezy)
__Taking aspirin
__Certain foods (eggs, nuts, milk, etc.)
__House dust (when someone dusts or vacuums)
__Outdoor dust (blowing dust on windy days)

__Molds (mildew, damp or musty basements, etc.)

__Pollens (trees, weeds, grasses)

__Strong smells (paint, glue, perfume, sprays, soaps, gasoline, etc.)

__Smoke (cigars, cigarettes, pipes, candles, campfires, etc.)

__Air pollution (including car exhaust)

__Weather (hot, cold, windy, dry, fast changing)

__Cold air

__Animals (especially cats, but also dogs, horses, birds, etc.)

__Seeing somebody else have trouble breathing

Caution

Something that seems to be a trigger can turn out not to be one at all. It might be *connected* to a trigger instead. For example, suppose you put a check mark next to "getting upset" because you remember feeling angry right before you felt wheezy. Maybe you got into a fight or a shouting match when you were angry. It may turn out that the physical exertion of the fight is what triggered your asthma rather than the angry feelings. You might try to remember times when you got angry and just sat quietly. Did you get asthma then?

Go back over your list of triggers, and for each one you checked ask yourself, "Was there anything else, any other trigger, going on at the same time that might have been the real cause of the attack?" If so, put a question mark next to that trigger.

Ask people in your family whether they think the "question mark" triggers give you asthma. Tell them to think carefully, just as you did, and to describe specific times they remember noticing the triggers at work. People often have different ideas about what causes an asthma attack.

Another way to figure out your triggers is to keep a simple asthma diary. Put a tablet of paper and a pencil or pen where you will see them when you are getting ready for bed. Before you go to sleep, try to remember if you had any tightness or wheezing during the day, and when and where you first noticed it. Write that down. (You don't have to remember exactly, just do the best you can.) If you had a full-blown asthma attack, write that down.

Next, write down the trigger you think caused the tightness or wheezing or the attack. The trigger list in this book can help to jog your memory. If you can't think of a trigger, try to remember where you were and what you were doing during the half hour before you noticed the change in your breathing. Write down a trigger you think might have been present during that time. Don't be afraid to guess.

You and your family will soon notice two things. First, certain triggers keep coming up more often than others. You will want to concentrate on avoid-

ing or controlling those triggers. Second, certain guesses will keep coming up over and over. Chances are they'll turn out to be real triggers.

You might also take your trigger list and diary with you to your next doctor's appointment. Your doctor will be very pleased to see that you are working so hard to learn your triggers, and he or she may be able to help you more clearly identify them and suggest ways to control your exposure to them.

Avoiding Your Asthma Triggers

As you accumulate your list of triggers, think about ways you can avoid them. Use your imagination. Ask your family for suggestions. Ask your doctor. If you have friends with asthma, ask them if they've tried anything that helps their asthma and see if it can work for you, too. Every time you think of a way to avoid a trigger, write it down. You'll soon discover that by avoiding triggers, you'll have fewer and less severe attacks. Here are some possible triggers and some things you can do about them. As you get better at spotting and avoiding your triggers, you'll get better at preventing asthma attacks.

Trigger: Exercise and Overexertion
What to Do About It:
- Warm up before you start to play. Start your activity slowly or in small amounts until you feel you are ready and able to do more. Stretching is also a good way to warm up. So are practice swings and throws.
- Take frequent rest breaks during a game so that you can avoid getting out of breath. Find other activities—such as reading, music, video games, darts, pool, chess, puzzles, or stamp collecting—

that you can do when you don't feel up to something more strenuous. Ask your family for suggestions, too.

- If your doctor says it's okay, take extra or special medication on days when you know you're going to be playing hard.

Trigger: Animals
What to Do About It:

- If a friend with furry pets invites you over, suggest instead that the friend come to your house.
- When you are going to visit people who have an animal, ask (or have your parents ask) before your visit if they can keep the animal in another room while you're there.
- If you want a pet to care for, try one without fur or feathers, such as a tropical fish.
- If your doctor says it's okay, take extra medicine before you visit somebody who has a pet.

Trigger: Cold Weather
What to Do About It:

- Breathe through your nose as much as possible so that the air is warmed by the time it reaches your trachea and bronchi.
- Do things indoors on especially cold days.

- Wear a muffler or ski mask so that you don't breathe a lot of cold air.

Trigger: Getting Angry
What to Do About It:
- When people annoy you and you feel angry, speak up but don't shout.
- If you know that getting angry may bring on an asthma attack, ask yourself if a situation that is bothering you is worth the risk. That may help you let it go.
- Wait until you've calmed down a little before discussing the problem. You'll be better able to control yourself and avoid an argument.
- Try to talk about what's on your mind rather than getting physical.

Trigger: Catching a Cold
What to Do About It:
- Avoid getting too close to people with a cold or the flu, if possible.
- Wash your hands often to protect yourself from germs.
- Tell your family right away when you feel a cold coming on. They will help you treat colds and coughs as soon as possible, hopefully before the symptoms become bad enough to trigger asthma.

Trigger: Cigarette and Cigar Smoke
What to Do About It:

- Talk to your family about having and enforcing a "No Smoking" policy in your house. Remember, it's everyone's right to breathe smoke-free air.
- When you are outdoors, move away when people are smoking.
- If asking someone not to smoke makes you uncomfortable, ask your parents or other family members to make the request for you.
- Avoid rooms and buildings where people smoke or are permitted to smoke. Choose restaurants and other businesses that have a smoke-free policy.
- If people are smoking and won't stop, leave the room.
- Don't smoke yourself! Say *NO!* if somebody offers you a cigarette.

Trigger: Foods
What to Do About It:

- Ask your doctor and your parents which foods (cereals, bread, candies, etc.) are bad for you. Make a list, and avoid eating those foods.
- Read the ingredients on boxes and wrappers before you eat what's inside. If you have trouble reading the ingredients or you don't know which ingredients to avoid, ask your family for help.
- When you go to school and parties, take treats that are okay for you to eat. Take enough to share with others.

Trigger: House Dust

Dust is a problem for people with asthma. Dust contains things like mold and dust mites, which are tiny creatures you can only see with a microscope. Dust mites can be found in mattresses, pillows, clothes, bedding, towels, rugs, and stuffed animals. Dust can make your asthma worse. Talk to your parents and other family members about the dust in your house and develop a plan. You will all need to work together to reduce dust. Here are some suggestions.

What to Do About It:

- Use a damp cloth to dust furniture so particles don't get distributed into the air.
- Wash all bedding once a week in hot water.
- Put special dust-proof covers on your pillow and mattress.
- Purchase a dehumidifier, which will dry out the air, killing dust mites.
- Think about getting a HEPA air cleaner for your room to filter out many dust mites.
- Don't jump on furniture or beds. Jumping stirs up dust particles.
- If you need something from a dusty place, ask somebody to get it for you.
- Carpets and rugs harbor dust. It is best not to have them in your home. If you do have rugs, washable cotton is best. If you have carpets that can't be removed, vacuum them frequently.
- Wood and tile floors are much less dust-friendly than carpet. This is something for your parents to consider when choosing and decorating living space for the family.

Trigger: Strong Smells
What to Do About It:
- Tell people in your family if you are bothered by strong odors from perfumes, aerosol sprays, cleansers, glue, or other products that they use. When family members know you are sensitive, they can avoid certain products, use them when you are not around, or tell you beforehand so that you can go into another room or leave the house altogether.
- If your house is going to be painted, have your parents make arrangements for you to stay at a friend or relative's house until the smell is gone.
- Ask your family to buy unscented versions of such products as soaps and deodorants.
- If your family needs to use an insecticide such as roach or ant spray, which can irritate your airways, stay out of the house when it is used and until the smell wears off.

Trigger: Pollens
Trees, weeds, and grasses produce microscopic pollen grains that float in the air at certain times of the year, depending on the plant. These pollens can be very bad for your asthma. If your doctor has told you which pollens are bad for you and when they are likely to be in the air, try to be careful at those times. For example, tree pollens are heavy in the spring, and late summer to fall is the period for ragweed—a wild plant that grows in abundance and produces an extremely irritating pollen. These periods of heavy pollen are known as allergy seasons.

What to Do About It:

- Play indoors rather than outdoors during allergy seasons that are bothersome for you.
- If your house has an air filtering system, have someone in your family turn it on or make sure that it is turned on.
- Keep windows closed during allergy seasons.
- Mowing the lawn should not be one of your chores. Mowing may look like fun, but grass pollen and particles can trigger an asthma attack.
- Find out what the "pollen count" is each day, so that you'll know when you need to be careful. Pollen counts are reported on local radio stations, in local newspapers, on television, and on the Internet (see page 80). Ask your family to help you get this information.

Trigger: Air Pollution

What to Do About It:

- Make it a habit to listen for air quality readings during the news on local radio and television stations each morning. Air pollution alerts are issued by local public health agencies when air pollution reaches a dangerous level. Stay indoors on pollution-alert days.
- Avoid power lawn mowers, leaf blowers, go-carts, and other small engines that often release pollutants into the air.
- Avoid walking along busy streets where air pollution from cars is heaviest.
- If possible, keep car windows up and use air con-

ditioning when you are riding in heavy traffic.

- Smoke from fires can be extremely irritating and quickly trigger an attack. Have your parents use a gas grill rather than a charcoal grill. Never burn leaves or trash. Besides triggering asthma, it is usually illegal. Avoid campfires, especially when they are being started and put out, which is when they produce the most smoke.

Healthy Habits for Body and Mind

In addition to knowing and avoiding your triggers, you can help yourself get better control of your asthma by following a few general healthy habits for your body and mind.

A Healthy Body

Most important: Try to stay healthy and in good shape. Besides taking your prescribed medicines on time and following your doctor's advice, that also means eating properly, exercising appropriately, and getting enough sleep.

- Eating properly means choosing foods that are good for you and staying away from foods that are bad for you. This sounds simple, but many people do not know which foods are healthy, or how to prepare them in a healthy way. Ask your doctor for guidelines on good nutrition for you and your family. Learn about the Food Pyramid. Choose snacks like pretzels, yogurt, and fruit instead of chips and cookies. Drink water, milk, and juice; stay away from soft drinks.
- The right kind and amount of physical activity helps keep us healthy. We have discovered that

What we should eat each day:

sweets,
Fats, Oil.
(use sparingly)

Eat less of
this stuff!

Milk,
Yogurt,
cheese.
(2-3 servings)

Meat, Poultry,
Fish, Eggs, Nuts,
Dried beans.
(2-3 servings)

Veggies
(3-5 servings)

Fruit
(2-4 servings)

chomp

Eat
most from
down here.

Bread, Pasta,
Rice, Cereals.
(6-11 servings)

"Eat less at the Top, more at the bottom."

people who spend many hours seated at a desk
or the computer or the TV have immune systems
that don't work as well as other people's do. As
you learned in this book, your immune system
plays a major role in your asthma. In addition to
just feeling better, stronger, and more energetic,
you'll be helping your asthma if you find several
ways to be active that are sensible for you.

- How much sleep do you need? Some experts say
  a minimum of eight hours a night, and others say
  that kids may need even more. Ask your doctor
  for some guidelines to make sure that you are
  getting enough, and pay attention to when you
  feel tired.

Positive Thinking

In addition to general care of your body, spend time
thinking about and imagining how your life would
be better with your asthma under control. Remind
yourself that through understanding and practice,
you can improve your asthma. Although you have an

illness that requires treatment and isn't likely to go away, you really can learn ways to help yourself stay well. Positive thinking leads to positive results. The first step to achieving a goal is often to visualize ourselves doing it. Picture yourself the way you want to be. You can do it!

Minimizing Stress

Finally, try to keep your stress level down. If things worry or upset you, see what you can do about them so they aren't on your mind. Here are some suggestions for dealing with your worries:

- Talking about your concerns with your family or somebody else that you trust is one of the best ways to feel better.
- It may help to keep a journal where you can talk through your worries.
- Be sure that somebody at home and at school knows what to do in case you want help in handling an asthma attack. You'll feel more secure when you know that there is somebody you can turn to if necessary.
- Learn and practice the relaxation techniques described in chapter 6 to feel less stressed.

Early Warning Signs

Nobody can avoid all of their triggers all the time. Therefore, another very important technique for controlling asthma is to spot attacks when they are first getting started and to treat them right away. Minutes, hours, sometimes even days before an attack, asthma sends out a signal—an early warning sign, or "EWS"— that an attack is on its way. When you know what these early warning signs are, you are more likely to notice them and be able to respond before the attack starts or gets worse.

Remember, you're in charge, but you're not alone. Your family members can make it easier for you to notice an asthma attack coming on. For instance, they might notice that you look pale or tired before you are aware of it. Talk to them about how you would like them to let you know when they think they see an early warning sign.

Most Common Early Warning Signs of Asthma
Getting more out of breath than usual
- You usually go up the stairs at home or school without any trouble, but this time you feel tired or you have to stop to catch your breath.
- You have to pause for breath frequently while you're talking on the phone.
- You run out of breath before you can finish reading a sentence out loud.

Feeling sweaty or getting sudden chills even though you don't seem to have a cold
- Someone asks you if you're feeling sick when you think you're feeling fine.
- You think your house or classroom feels over-heated when no one else does.
- You feel overdressed or underdressed, even though the weather hasn't changed.

Feeling edgy or uptight for no reason
Usually you know why you feel edgy. You might have an exam coming up, or you have to perform in front of an audience, or you have a problem with a friend. But if you're feeling edgy or uptight and don't know why, it could be an EWS that your breathing has begun to change.

Fast or shallow breathing
Your breathing normally speeds up when you exert

yourself because you need more oxygen and have more carbon dioxide to get rid of. However, if you notice that your breathing is faster or more shallow than usual, but you haven't been exerting yourself, it could be an EWS.

Sleeping restlessly or getting tired more easily
- Even though you slept all night, you wake up feeling tired.
- You wake up in the middle of the night, although you are usually a sound sleeper.
- Your schoolbag feels like it weighs a ton.
- Someone tells you that you look like you haven't slept or that you have dark circles under your eyes, even though you had a good night's sleep.
- Somebody in your family notices you tossing and turning, even though you don't wake up.
- You have unusually bad dreams.

Hunching over
During an asthma attack, people often bend over and rest their hands on a tabletop or the back of a chair. It seems to help them breathe. If you find

yourself hunched over and you aren't having an attack, it could be an EWS that your breathing has started to change.

- You are standing with your hands in your back pockets or tucked into the back of your waistband.
- You look down at the ground more than usual when you are walking.
- You lean against things more than usual when you're talking to friends.
- People tell you that you're slouching.

Clearing your throat frequently
This usually means that you are accumulating mucus, or you feel that you are. Either way, your breathing does not feel right. It could be an EWS.

Coughing and sneezing
These EWSs, like throat clearing, probably mean that there is blockage somewhere in your respiratory system. You want to pay special attention to coughing and sneezing because they can be triggers as well as EWSs.

Funny feelings or noises in your chest or throat when you talk or breathe
- Your chest tickles or you feel that you want to cough when you take a deep breath.
- The back of your throat feels itchy.
- You hear rattles, gurgles, or squeaks when you breathe or talk.

Retractions

You can see what *retractions* are by looking in a mirror when you have an asthma attack. Look at the base of your throat just above where your collar bones come together. You'll see that when you inhale, the skin in that area gets pulled in. That's a retraction. It doesn't happen when you're breathing normally. Strictly speaking, retractions are not an early warning sign. They usually happen during an actual attack. However, some people get asthma so often that they may not pay attention to mild attacks. If you are one of these people, please don't wait for your symptoms to become severe. If you notice retractions when you look in the mirror, take action even if you don't think your breathing is bad.

Pursed-lips breathing

Pursed-lips breathing is exhaling through your mouth with your lips loosely pressed together. Like retractions, this form of breathing is not usually an early warning sign. It is something people do when they have an actual asthma attack because it helps them to breathe more easily. Please take pursed-lips breathing as a serious sign to act before your asthma gets worse.

What to Do About Early Warning Signs

With a little practice, you can become so good at spotting EWSs that you won't have to think about them very much. They'll catch your attention.

Here's how to practice. Every day for two or three weeks, take a moment to scan your body for

EWSs each time you pick up a book or use the telephone or your computer. This way you'll be checking several times a day. You'll be training your mind to notice changes when they happen.

When you notice an early warning sign, try any of these suggestions:

- Make sure you take your medicine on time.
- Check to see if you are being exposed to a trigger. If you are, do everything you can to minimize your exposure. (See the suggestions in chapter 3.)
- See if getting some fresh air helps.
- Try drinking something warm.
- Take extra medicine if your doctor has told you to. If you don't have it with you, have somebody make you some strong coffee. The caffeine in coffee helps open your airways.
- Try slow abdominal breathing and/or a relaxation exercise. (See chapter 6.)
- Use a peak-flow meter.

Peak-Flow Meter

A *peak-flow meter* is a device that tells you how well your upper airways are working. You breathe into it, and it measures how fast you can breathe out. *Peak flow* is the maximum, or peak, amount of air that you breathe out when you are not affected by your asthma. As asthma gets worse, peak-flow (P-F) measurements drop.

If your doctor has trained you to use a P-F meter and you have one at home, you have a great early warning system. If you spot an early warning sign,

Read the number

800

400

100

meter goes up

Blow here

take a P-F reading and see if your breathing has begun to change.

If you don't know about P-F, ask your doctor. There are many different P-F meters available, and some of them are even small enough to carry in your pocket or book bag. Ask your doctor to help you choose one that's good for you.

Ask your doctor to help you make a plan of what to do when you spot an EWS. With your ability to spot early warning signs, a plan of action, and the skills you are learning and practicing, you will gain more control over your asthma!

Relaxation Exercises 6

Many people with asthma have learned how to use breathing and relaxation exercises to stop tension from triggering and aggravating their asthma. Relaxing your body will help you to stay calm during an attack and do what is needed for your treatment. It will also help you to control strong emotions that can trigger your asthma.

Relaxing your breathing helps you in two ways. First, your airways stay warm and moist, the way they should be. Second, you breathe more easily when relaxed than when you try to force air in and out of your airways. If you've ever tried to blow through a straw, especially a soggy paper one, you know that the harder you blow, the more likely the straw is to collapse and stop air from passing through it. Your airways work the same way. The less you try to *force* air through them, the more air you'll get.

You are also going to learn how to change your thinking so you don't scare yourself or make yourself feel ashamed about your asthma. When you learn not to think about asthma as a scary enemy, you will find that it gets better and better.

How to Relax Your Body

Here are two relaxation exercises. The first exercise takes about ten minutes and requires you to lie or sit down. The second exercise takes only about one minute and can be done almost anywhere. Learning the ten-minute exercise well will make it possible for you to use the shorter one and still get good results.

Full-Body Relaxation (10 minutes)

Do this exercise in a quiet place and at a time when you are not likely to be interrupted. You may want to alert family members of your need for quiet time. Also, consider asking someone in your family to help you do the exercise correctly by reading you the following instructions and watching as you follow them.

Find a comfortable position lying on your back or sitting in a soft chair with your legs stretched out in front of you. If you wear glasses, remove them and loosen any tight-fitting clothes. Do the exercise with your eyes closed or in a place with soft lighting.

Tense and tighten all the muscles of your body from your toes all the way to the top

TIGHTEN

Then loosen up . . .

of your head. Curl your toes, flex your calves, tighten your thighs, make your back stiff, pull in your belly, make your arms stiff and straight, clench your fists, bite down hard, squeeze your eyes tight, and scrunch up your face. Hold the tightness and slowly count from 1 to 7 in your head while you concentrate on how your muscles feel.

At the count of 7, let go all at once, as if all that tightness is exploding out. Let your body become as limp as an overcooked noodle. Try to feel the tension draining out of your muscles. Help it by letting go. Feel the bed or the chair holding you up so you can let your muscles relax. Concentrate on the feeling of looseness.

Notice if any parts of your body start to feel pleasantly warm or heavy as they relax. Keep letting go until you think you're as relaxed as you can possibly be.

Next, in your mind, check the different muscles of your body. Start with your toes and slowly notice your way up to the top of your head. Do you sense any spots of tightness or tension, as you did when you purposely made your muscles tight? If you do, let the tightness in those places drain away, one spot at a time. As you practice, you'll learn which of your muscles tighten up most when you get tense. Those will be important to check and release when you want to relax.

When you've carefully checked your body and let go of as much tension as you think you can, try to picture yourself doing something that is very pleasant and relaxing, such as going for a walk, taking a warm bath, or lying in the sun. Try to pretend that you are doing it right now. As you do, slowly go over the muscles of your body one more time in your mind, and try to let go even more. Use the same imaginary scene each time you do the exercise. It will become a switch that you can use to turn on your relaxation response.

Now just take some time to enjoy being relaxed. Most people like to do this exercise when they go to bed, to help them fall asleep. If you get up after the exercise, try to stay relaxed.

Imagery Relaxation Exercise (1 to 2 minutes)
To prepare for this exercise, read the following descriptions. After you read each one, close your eyes and try to imagine the scene or event described. Hold the image for as long as you can, up to a count of 7, and then go on to the next image.

Try to imagine:

a beautiful golden sunset
snow falling gently to the ground
drifting in a rowboat on a warm summer day
sitting by a waterfall
listening to the falling rain
looking at a beautiful flower
the aroma of something delicious cooking or baking
waves rolling in and breaking on the beach
falling asleep when you are very tired
being as limp as a rag doll
listening to the wind blowing through the trees
sinking into a soft chair or bed
watching the clouds drift by on a warm summer day
drinking a glass of cool water when you're thirsty
entering a warm room on a cold, wintry day

After you've imaged all these scenes, pick the four that made you feel the most relaxed, or use your imagination to make up scenes of your own. Use these scenes when you want to relax but can't do the ten-minute exercise. Just close your eyes and picture each scene to a count of 7 as you let your body relax. With practice, you'll be able to do this exercise just about anywhere.

How to Relax Your Breathing
Abdominal Breathing
In chapter 1, we talked about your diaphragm, which is located inside your abdomen. When it pushes down and flattens out, air is sucked into your lungs. When it goes back up, air is pushed out

of your lungs. You always breathe with your diaphragm when you sleep.

However, like many people, you may have gotten into the habit of using your chest muscles for breathing when you are awake. This is not a good way to breathe, especially for people with asthma. Chest breathing is usually rapid and shallow. It can cool and irritate your airways and trigger or aggravate your asthma symptoms. The following exercise will help you learn to breathe with your diaphragm all the time.

First, lie down on your back or stretch out in a comfortable chair. (If you find it uncomfortable to lie on your back, then lie on your side with your knees pulled up a little.) If you're wearing tight clothes or a belt, loosen them. Place one hand on your belly with your pinkie just above your belly button. Place your other hand across your chest just below your collar bone.

Next, relax your shoulders and arms as much as you can and breathe normally. If the hand resting on your chest is moving up and down when you breathe in and out, you are using your chest muscles more than you should. You want to feel the

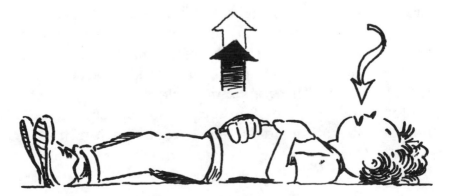

hand on your belly moving up and down as you breathe in and out, and the one on your chest moving hardly at all. If you find it difficult to breathe this way, the following suggestion may help.

Imagine that you have a balloon in your belly. When you breathe in, the balloon fills up so your belly puffs up and pushes your hand up. When you breathe out, the balloon empties out and your belly and hand go down. You can help this process by relaxing your belly and then trying to feel it filling up when you breathe in. Remember to keep your shoulders and arms relaxed. When you breathe out, you can squeeze more air out by tightening your belly just a little and then letting it relax again when you start to breathe in. Breathe slowly and easily. You don't have to take big, deep breaths, and you don't have to work hard.

As you practice, you'll learn how deep your breaths need to be for you to feel that you're getting enough air. This is a great exercise to do with a partner. Ask a family member to help by reading the directions and watching you breathe. Don't be discouraged if this exercise turns out to be harder than it sounds. Keep practicing. If you're still having trouble getting your abdomen to move after several practice sessions, try the following suggestion:

Get down on your hands and knees, resting your weight on your hands. Concentrate on how your belly feels as you breathe. You'll quickly notice that it feels like it's filling up and emptying out. Stay on all fours for a couple of minutes, and concentrate on how your breathing feels. Then practice again in a

lying or sitting position. Try to get the same feeling in your belly that you had when you were on all fours. With practice, you'll learn to do this exercise correctly.

By the way, until you're good at abdominal breathing, you can always get down on all fours when you want to breathe more easily. Many people with asthma have said that breathing in this position makes them feel more comfortable.

Practice abdominal breathing for five minutes a day until you think you know how to do it correctly. Try practicing after you've finished your relaxation exercise. Do the breathing exercise when lying down or sitting until you're good at it, then try it standing up. When you're good at that, try it while you walk slowly back and forth. Then try it walking at a normal speed. After a while, you are likely to get in the habit of breathing this way all the time. You are designed for abdominal breathing. If you breathe this way when you feel yourself getting asthma, you'll get more air without struggling.

Pursed-Lips Breathing
Remember that air moves more easily through a narrow tube if it is not being forced. During an asthma attack, your airways become narrowed because

of swelling, mucus, and muscle spasm. Slowing your breathing down, especially when you exhale, is important.

In chapter 5, you read about pursed-lips breathing. This kind of breathing is something people do almost automatically when they are having an asthma attack. However, if you are aware of it and do it deliberately, you can use this kind of breathing as a way to get more air with less effort.

When you breathe with pursed lips, you exhale through your mouth with your lips lightly pressed together. Because you are breathing against your lips, you can't breathe out fast. Try it. Don't blow hard. Breathe out as normally as you can. You'll notice that you get more air out and that your next breath is deeper and more satisfying.

When you feel yourself getting asthma, the powerful combination of relaxation exercises, abdominal breathing, and pursed-lips breathing will help you stay in control. At those times, remember that you also have your family, your doctor, and your medicine to turn to for help. Remember that every one of your attacks has always come to an end, and so will this one.

How to Relax Your Mind

Not being able to breathe easily is uncomfortable, but it doesn't have to be upsetting or scary. If you feel upset or scared when you have asthma, you may be thinking upsetting or scary thoughts. Or maybe you are angry, or embarrassed, or frustrated about your asthma.

Unfortunately, these feelings won't help you. They might even make your asthma feel worse. Having strong feelings makes your muscles get tight and use up more oxygen than when they are relaxed. Your lungs have to work harder to get that extra oxygen. You might breathe faster or harder and try to force air into your lungs.

Remember that trying to force air through narrowed airways makes it harder for the air to reach your lungs. This can also irritate your airways and make them shut down even more. As a result, your asthma will get more severe. But all that doesn't have to happen.

If you find yourself feeling upset or scared, ask yourself, "What am I thinking or imagining or remembering that is upsetting me?" It's important to ask yourself that question because people aren't always aware of what they are thinking about. For example, if your teacher gives you a lot of homework and you feel annoyed, you might not notice that you're thinking, "It's not fair! I hate doing homework! I wish I had a different teacher!" You just know that you're annoyed.

Try to be aware of your own thoughts. You'll soon

begin to notice that scared and upset feelings are accompanied by scary and upsetting thoughts and pictures in your mind. Here are some thoughts that may frighten or upset you:

- "I'm never going to get better."
- "I'm going to die."
- "What if my medicine doesn't work?"
- "I'm all alone. What if nobody helps me?"
- "People with asthma have to go to the hospital or get shots."
- "What if people find out I have asthma and don't want to be my friend?"
- "Why me? Nobody else I know has asthma!"
- "I hate being sick!"

Do any of these thoughts sound familiar? You may have other thoughts that upset or frighten you. Think about whether your fears are realistic or exaggerated. When you are afraid, it's easy to think the worst is going to happen. You can help your asthma by learning how to notice and ignore exaggerated thoughts, then substituting more reasonable ones. For example:

- "Very few people die of asthma if they take care of themselves, and I'm going to take very good care of myself."
- "People will help me if I ask them to."
- "Everyone has some problems. My problem happens to be asthma. So what? It could have been something worse."

- "It doesn't help to hate anything. It's better to do something about it, and that's exactly what I'm going to do about my asthma."
- "I know what to do about my asthma, so I don't have to be afraid of it."
- "My friends will like me even if they know I have asthma. If I don't make a big deal out of it, they won't either."

Try sharing this list with family members, and ask them to remind you to think more positive thoughts if they notice you are worrying about your asthma.

Asthma Medicines

Asthma medicines are now better than ever. That's because, over time, doctors have learned new things about asthma. The more that doctors understand about the causes of asthma, the closer they come to finding a cure for it. In chapter 1, you read about a surprising new discovery: Children who go to nursery school have asthma less than children who don't. Such findings are clues. Doctors are always searching for new clues so that they can help people with asthma live more normal, active, and happy lives.

Doctors use several different kinds of medicines to treat asthma. At first you might think that asthma medicines are a little confusing. If so, ask your doctor or someone in your family to explain them to you. Your doctor and family can also help you do a good job of using medicines correctly.

Asthma medicines do two things:

1   They relax the muscles in your airways when you get symptoms so you can breathe more easily
2   They prevent symptoms by keeping the inflammation in your airways under control.

Most asthma medicines do one or the other of these jobs, and some of them seem to do a little of both.

Controlling Symptoms

The medicines that relax and open your airways are called *bronchodilators*. There are several kinds. They come as a spray or powder that you inhale, or as a liquid or tablet that you swallow. Bronchodilators start to give you relief in minutes. The most common side effects are jittery, irritable, or restless feelings; fast heartbeat; headaches; cramps; and nausea. If you get any of these side effects, tell your doctor. You may need a different medicine, a smaller dose, or a different schedule for taking it. Most people lose these side effects after using the bronchodilators for several days.

Be careful how you use bronchodilator inhalers. They make you feel better quickly, so you might think it's okay to use them whenever you feel your symptoms are coming on. But if you inhale more than eight puffs a day, you could be taking too much and not getting the help you need to control the inflammation in your lungs. THAT'S NOT A GOOD IDEA! If you are using bronchodilators a lot, tell your doctor. Together you'll find a better way to control your symptoms.

Controlling Inflammation

The medicines that are used to control airway inflammation are cromolyn, nedocromil, a new class of medicines called leukotriene antagonists, and steroids. They do not relax the airway muscles quickly, as bronchodilators do, so they can't (and shouldn't) be used to get quick relief in the event of an attack. They are used to prevent attacks. Cromolyn and nedocromil are inhaled as gas-propelled sprays or in powder form. Their only side effect for most people is a bad taste, which you can get rid of quickly by rinsing your mouth. Leukotriene antagonist medicine is taken as a tablet one or two times a day.

Steroids are taken by mouth in spray, pill, or liquid form, or they may be injected. Steroids can have side effects such as weight gain, roundness of the face, or mood changes. However, doctors have found ways to reduce those side effects. If you take steroids, your doctor needs to know how you're doing at all times, so be sure that you don't skip appointments.

Also, never stop taking steroids without your doctor's instructions. Your body needs to have steroids available at all times. Normally, your body manufactures its own steroids. When you take steroid medicines, your body temporarily shuts down its own production. It takes time for it to start up again. If you stop taking steroids suddenly, your body is left without a very important protection. You have to reduce steroid medicines slowly, to give your body time to start producing them again.

Preventing Inflammation

Bronchodilators control the symptoms of asthma attacks. Cromolyn, nedocromil, leukotriene antagonists, and steroids control the inflammation that triggers those attacks. Now doctors are working on new medicines that are designed to prevent the inflammation in the first place. Those medicines will work by controlling the substances in your body that make you likely to develop inflammation.

For example, people with asthma seem to have a lot more of a substance called IgE (pronounced "eye-gee-ee") than people who don't. IgE is a chemical in your body that is important in the normal immune response. Too much of it, however, seems to be one of the keys in making asthmatic airways get inflamed. Doctors are now working toward testing an "anti-IgE"—a medicine that may help to normalize the amount of IgE in your body. Other medicines of the future are in the works. Someday, they may make asthma a thing of the past.

How Much Do You Need?

People need different amounts of medicine to control their asthma. If your asthma is mild, you may need to take medicine only when your symptoms act up. If your asthma is severe, you may need to use several different medicines every day.

If you get attacks in the middle of the night or with exercise, your doctor can prescribe long-acting medicines to help prevent them. You take these medicines before you go to sleep, and their effects last through the night.

Your asthma is mild if:
- You have no more than one or two episodes of coughing or wheezing a week.
- You are able to exercise moderately without getting symptoms.
- You rarely miss school.
- You wake up in the middle of the night with symptoms no more than one or two times a month.
- You use bronchodilators less than one time per week.

Your asthma is moderate if:
- You have more than one or two episodes of coughing or wheezing a week.
- You cough or wheeze regularly with exercise.
- You wake up at night frequently.
- You have occasional but not frequent severe attacks.
- You had to visit your doctor or the hospital for emergency treatment three to six times in the past year.
- You have to use bronchodilators two to three times per week and steroid inhalers routinely.

Your asthma is severe if:
- You wheeze almost every day.
- You have frequent severe attacks.
- You are unable to exercise without wheezing.
- Your sleep is interrupted every night.
- You have to visit the doctor or emergency room more than six times a year.

- You have been hospitalized more than two times in the past year.
- You have fainted during attacks.
- You have required daily bronchodilators and inhaled or oral steroids.

   Your doctor will decide which medicine is right for you, and how much of it you should take. Taking less than what is prescribed without consulting your doctor is NOT a good idea. If you have side effects or other problems with your medicine, be sure to discuss them with your doctor.

Inhalers and Nebulizers

If any of the medicines you take are the kind you inhale, you use either an *inhaler* or a *nebulizer*.
   An inhaler, sometimes called a metered dose

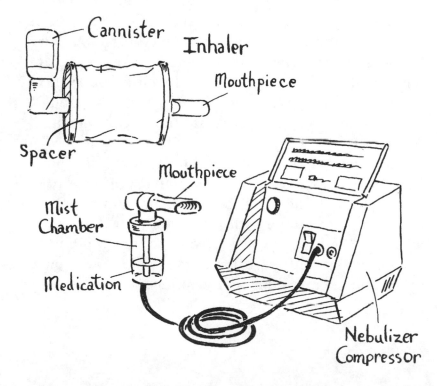

Cannister

Inhaler

Mouthpiece

Spacer

Mouthpiece

Mist Chamber

Medication

Nebulizer Compressor

inhaler or MDI, is a small metal canister with a mouthpiece at one end. When you squeeze the canister, it sends a gas-propelled spray of medicine into the mouthpiece, and you breathe it in. Newer medications contain a fine powder that is directly inhaled without pressurized gas. These can be the easiest and most efficient medicines to use, and some have longer lasting effects, lasting twelve or more hours.

Some inhalers come with a spacer, which is a chamber that fits onto the mouthpiece. The spacer catches and holds the spray so that you can inhale it more effectively.

It takes a lot of practice to take medicine properly with an inhaler. You inhale the medicine slowly and then hold your breath so that the medicine can settle into your lungs. Your doctor will show you how to do this.

A nebulizer is a machine with an air compressor that turns liquid medicine into a mist that you can breathe in through a mouthpiece. Unlike an inhaler, which delivers the whole dose of medicine in one spray, a nebulizer creates a little bit of mist each time you take a breath, so a treatment can take a few minutes.

Your doctor will show you how to use your inhaler or nebulizer, and should check to be sure that you are doing it right. You might want to ask a family member to be with you when your doctor explains the proper way to use it, so that you have someone to practice with at home. You'll catch on more quickly and do it right sooner.

Taking Your Medicine

Most people use their medicine properly because they know that it will help them feel better. When people don't use their medicine properly, some common explanations are:

"I forgot."

"I wasn't sure which medicine to take."

"I was feeling okay. I didn't think I needed any."

If any of these reasons sounds familiar, this next section is for you. Here are some typical problems that people have with taking medicines, followed by some suggestions for solving them.

You don't understand your doctor's instructions.
Ask questions. If you can't, get somebody in your family to do it for you. Doctors are busy and may not take the time to explain things. Doctors work with asthma every day, so things that are complicated to you may seem simple to them. If you ask a question or say "I didn't understand that," you'll let your doctor know you need more of an explanation.

Your family believes it's better to take less medicine no matter what.
Have a family member meet with your doctor so that he or she will understand why you need to take the amount of medicine that has been prescribed. Also, ask your family to read this chapter.

Your medicine tastes bad.
Rinse your mouth after you take it. The bad taste lasts only a moment, but the relief lasts a long time.

Your family believes that asthma can be cured without using medicine.
Chances are, somebody has given them one of the false ideas you'll read about in the next chapter. This book suggests many ways for you to help control your asthma. Using medicine is one of the most effective ways.

You don't know how to use your nebulizer or inhaler properly.
Ask your doctor or your pharmacist to show you how. Ask him or her to practice with you until you feel sure you've got it right. It isn't difficult, but it can be tricky at first.

You get side effects from your medicine, like trembly feelings, cramps, or a hoarse voice.
Report the symptoms to your doctor. He or she may be able to reduce the side effects. They often wear off as your body gets used to the medicine.

You are embarrassed to take asthma medicine in front of other people, or other kids sometimes tease you when you take it.
- Show your inhaler to your friends when you don't need to use it. Explain what it does and how it works. People often get uneasy when they see something they don't understand and cover it up by teasing or making jokes.
- If you have a health education class, ask your teacher to do a session on asthma. You may even volunteer to explain your medicines.

- When you have to take your medicine or use your inhaler, say, "It's time to fill my tank." If you take your medicine with a smile, other people will probably start to treat it lightly also.
- If someone is mean or teases you when you take your medicine, ignore him or her, or look the person in the eye and calmly say something like, "You're bothering me. Please stop." Practice being assertive in your imagination or with someone in your family so you'll be ready.

You worry that your family is spending too much money on your medicines.
Remember that skipping your medicine could land you in the hospital emergency room, and that could be even more expensive. Also, remember that you and your health are valuable and worth it!

Others in your family don't take care of their health.
Keep in mind that you are your own person. You can choose to have good health habits, even if the people around you make different kinds of choices. Think about how your life will be better when you take the best possible care of yourself.

You are discouraged about your asthma.
Tell your doctors. Unless you tell them, they may think you're doing well and see no reason to try something different. Or, if you skip your medicine and don't tell them, they may think your asthma is worse than it is. They might restrict you in ways that aren't necessary. When you tell your doctors what is

on your mind or what is happening, you will get the treatment you need.

Some Very Important Things to Remember
When you get an attack you must start treatment very quickly, especially if:

- You've been to the emergency room three or more times during the last year.
- You've been hospitalized two or more times during the last year.
- You've been hospitalized or to the emergency room during the last month.
- You are taking steroids by mouth. (Ask your doctor if you aren't sure.)
- You've ever had to be in the Intensive Care Unit (ICU) of the hospital.
- You've ever fainted during an attack.

Always have emergency numbers for your doctor, the hospital, and the ambulance service available in case you need help. You can also call 911 in an emergency. Tell the operator your name, where you are, that you are having a bad asthma attack, and that you need help fast. The operator will know what to do to get you help quickly.

False Ideas About Asthma

Many people have ideas about asthma that doctors have now proven to be false. It is important that you understand why these ideas are not true so that you can take the best possible care of yourself. Read the list to people in your family. They may be surprised to find that they have some false ideas about asthma!

False idea #1: Asthma is an emotional problem that you can make up your mind not to have.
The truth is that asthma is not in people's minds. Asthma is as real as an infection, a cut, or a cavity in your tooth. You can't decide not to have it. Emotions can trigger or aggravate asthma, but they cannot make a person who doesn't have it get it.

False idea #2: Asthma can be cured by moving to a dry climate.
The truth is that moving to a dry climate can help some people. However, it can make asthma worse for others! People shouldn't plan such a move without discussing it with a doctor who knows their case thoroughly.

False idea #3: You will outgrow your asthma, so you don't need to treat it carefully.
The truth is that asthma can go away for days, weeks, and even years. However, the possibility that it will come back is always there. When it does, it needs to be treated with medicine and the self-help techniques that you are learning. In the meantime, treat your asthma with care.

False idea #4: Drink lots of liquids during an attack.
The truth is that this may satisfy your thirst, but it will probably not help you get over an attack any faster. Drink a reasonable amount, but don't count on water, tea, or juice to help you without medicine.

False idea #5: Breathing steam when you have an attack is as good as taking medicine.
The idea here is that breathing moist air into your lungs will help clear out mucus. This may be true. However, the medicine your doctor prescribes is also important. Don't substitute steam for medicine. Use both.

False idea #6: You should breathe into a paper bag during an attack.
This false idea is based on the fact that when peo-

ple get tense they start to breathe more quickly or deeply than they need to. Breathing into a paper bag at such times can help them calm down. However, it is not a treatment for asthma. Relaxing, abdominal breathing, pursed-lips breathing, and taking your medicine are more likely to help.

False idea #7: Over-the-counter medicines that you can buy without a doctor's prescription are as good as the medicines your doctor prescribes.
You've probably seen ads for such medicines. They show somebody having an asthma attack, taking the medicine, and then looking healthy and happy. Over-the-counter medicines may be cheaper and they may work for occasional mild attacks, but if your asthma is serious enough that you need to see a doctor, then you need the medicines your doctor prescribes. In fact, it may even be dangerous for you to use an over-the-counter medicine for asthma without your doctor's permission.

False idea #8: Asthma is inherited.
The truth is that the *tendency* to develop asthma is inherited. What it takes to turn that tendency into actual asthma is not known. That means that nobody is to blame for giving you asthma. It also means that having asthma is not a reason for you to worry about having children of your own someday.

Talking to Your Doctor

If you want to get the most out of your visits with your doctor, be prepared to do two things:

1 Answer your doctor's questions as best you can.
2 Ask your doctor questions about any part of your treatment you don't understand.

Your doctor sees you only once in a while and needs information from you in order to know how you have been doing. You need information from your doctor about how to take care of your asthma, and you need to clearly understand that information before you leave your doctor's office. Here are some suggestions on how to get the most out of your visit to the doctor.

Answer Your Doctor's Questions

Put your knowledge of early warning signs to use. When your doctor asks how you've been doing, be specific. For example, say that you've been coughing, feeling tight, sneezing, getting out of breath easily, noticing retractions, or waking up at night instead of saying, "I've been having some asthma." If you learn to think in terms of EWSs, you will be more aware of how you are doing, and you'll remem-

ber events to share with your doctor.

Take your asthma diary with you to the doctor's office or the hospital emergency room. What you have written in your diary will help you remember important details about your asthma, just as taking notes in class helps you remember what was discussed. Without your diary, you may remember severe attacks, but you are likely to forget how many small episodes you had, what triggered them, what you did about them, how long they lasted, and so on. Your doctor would like to have all of that important information.

If you have a peak-flow meter and have been using it, tell your doctor what your readings have been. Together with the information in your asthma diary, your P-F readings

Hint!

Before you go to the emergency room, try to reach your doctor over the phone (or have your parents call) and explain what's happening. Your doctor may be able to advise you and your family about what to do at home and save you a trip to the hospital.

will give your doctor a good picture of how you've been doing with your asthma.

If you have taken your medicines as your doctor prescribed, tell your doctor. He or she has a record of the medicines prescribed for you and will be able to find out quickly what you have been taking and how often. However, if you have skipped or added medicine, your doctor needs to know that too. The easiest way to keep track of changes you make in how you take your medicine is to write them down in your asthma diary (for example, "skipped 2:00 spray" or "used spray 4 times today"). Don't be afraid to tell your doctor about skipping or adding medi-cine. Your doctor is interested in keeping you healthy, not in grading your behavior!

Ask Your Doctor Questions

Your doctor will be glad to answer your questions about your asthma treatment. If you feel shy about asking questions, have a parent or other family

member ask the doctor for you. Here are some
examples of ways to ask questions when you don't
understand what your doctor tells you.

"What does .... mean?"

"Could you explain .... again?"

"Did you mean I should .... ?"

"You said .... , right?"

Here are some examples of ways to ask questions
when you want more information from your doctor
about your medicine.

"What is .... supposed to do?"

"How soon will it start to work?"

"How will I know if it's working?"

"Are there any side effects I should watch out for?"

"Is there anything I can do to help it work better?"

Ask your doctor if there is an asthma education
program in your area. The local Lung Association
often sponsors such programs. You and your family
can learn more by attending one.

When you think of questions between visits to
the doctor, write them down in your asthma diary.
As you pay more attention to controlling your
asthma, you will probably have more questions for
your doctor.

A New You

As you read about and practice the techniques described in this book, you will probably notice changes in how you think, feel, and act about your asthma. If your asthma has frightened or depressed you, you will probably start to feel more confident and in control. Friends and relatives may tell you that you seem better. You *are* better!

Here's a list of typical changes that people report. As you read through it, rate yourself on how much change you've experienced (0 = no change, 1 = a little bit of change, 2 = I'm getting there, 3 = I've got that one licked).

What You've Learned

__You can visualize and explain how your respiratory system works both normally and during an asthma attack.

__You know your asthma triggers or how to find out what they are.

__You know ways to avoid your triggers as much as possible.

__You know how to try to head off an attack when you've been exposed to one of your triggers.

__You know the early warning signs (EWSs).

__You notice when you have scary thoughts about asthma and know how to substitute positive or calming thoughts.

__You understand the false ideas that people have about asthma.

__You understand what asthma medicines do.

__You understand the problems you have with taking medicine and what to do about them.

__You know whom to call and what to say when you need help fast.

__You understand and believe from your experience that you and your doctor, working together, can control your asthma.

What You Feel

__You don't feel surprised or overwhelmed when you get symptoms.

__You stay calm during an attack.

__You feel comfortable about people knowing that you have asthma and seeing you take medicine.

__You feel secure because you know that you can get help when you need it.

__You feel eager to try activities that you thought you couldn't do.

__Your mood is upbeat more of the time.

__You feel good about yourself even though you have asthma.

How You Act

__You keep an asthma diary.

__You use your peak-flow meter to check out early warning signs.

__You write down any changes you make in how you take your medicine.

__You take your asthma diary with you to your doctor's office or the emergency room.

__You avoid your triggers whenever possible and take appropriate action when you can't.

__You recognize early warning signs (EWSs) and react appropriately when you spot one.

__You take your medicine regularly.

__You use your inhaler and nebulizer skillfully.

__You are prepared to answer and ask questions when you contact your doctor.

__You are more active even while you keep your asthma under control.

__You are good at relaxing and breathing with your diaphragm.

__You use pursed-lips breathing when you need to.

__You speak up when someone teases you about your asthma.

__You smile more!

As you become more familiar and comfortable with these techniques, you may want to rate yourself again. The more you practice, the more 3s you will have on your list, and the more control you will have over your asthma.

Hint!
From time to time, go back and read the questions on pages 15-16. They will help you see how much progress you've made.

Good luck, and breathe easy!

Guide for Parents

More than 25 years ago, health care professionals recognized the importance of involving children with asthma and their families in the management of the disease. Since then, we have learned that children, even very young ones, can limit both the impact and severity of their illness by learning simple skills that prevent and control attacks. As a result, many asthma self-management training programs have been developed and put to use in communities around the country.

Breathe Easy is the outgrowth of one of those programs, SUPER STUFF, which I developed in conjunction with the American Lung Association. SUPER STUFF differed from other programs in that it was designed to be self-teaching and usable at home. I took this approach because, for many children, classroom programs are either unavailable or too inconvenient. The information in SUPER STUFF was simple, interesting, and entertaining. As we expected, children and their families responded positively. After learning the skills, they reported feeling more confident and having fewer asthma-related problems. Children also missed fewer days of school because of their asthma.

Breathe Easy has also been written for children to read and use on their own. However, throughout the book I have suggested to children that they invite you and other family members to help them learn and practice asthma self-management. There are two important ways in which you can help. First, you can learn along with your child so that you can answer questions and help your child practice the exercises in the book. Second, you can reinforce your child's learning as he or she tries to make self-management a new habit.

Learning Along With Your Child

You probably already know a great deal about asthma and its management. However, there may still be areas of asthma management that you would like to learn more about. The questions that follow will help you to identify those areas and point you to the sections of this book that deal with them. By learning as much as you can about asthma, you will feel better equipped to guide your child toward a better understanding and more skillful management of the disease.

- Can you describe the working parts of the respiratory system and how they function in normal breathing? (See pages 9-11.)
- Do you know what changes take place in your child's respiratory system during an asthma attack? (See pages 11-13.)
- Can you name your child's asthma triggers? (See pages 17-19.)
- Do you know how you and your child can find out what triggers your child's asthma? (See pages 19-21.)
- How have you tried to eliminate asthma triggers from your home? How about things outside the home to which your child is allergic? (See pages 22-29.)
- Can you describe the early warning signs that tell you your child is starting to develop an asthma attack? (See pages 34-37.)
- Does your child know the early warning signs and how to spot them? (See pages 34-38.)
- When your child has an asthma attack, do you know how to help your child relax and breathe properly? (See pages 40-51.)
- Is your child afraid of asthma? Do you know what his or her scary thoughts are? Are you scared? Do you know how to help change scary thoughts into positive,

reassuring ones? (See pages 49-51.)
- What medicine(s) does your child take, and how are they supposed to help? (See pages 52-58.)
- What problems, if any, does your child have regarding his or her medicine? (See pages 59-62.)
- What problems, if any, do you or other family members have regarding your child's medicine? (See pages 59-62.)
- What problems does your child have at school or with friends because of asthma? Do you feel confident making suggestions about how to handle those problems? (See pages 60-61.)
- Do you believe that the teachers and staff at school understand asthma and how to handle it at school? Do you know what problems they have regarding asthma attacks that happen at school? (See pages 61-62.)
- Do you leave visits to the doctor feeling that you have gotten clear instructions? Do you and your child feel free to ask questions? (See pages 65-69.)
- Do you know where you can get the latest information about asthma and its treatment? (See pages 78-80.)

Reinforcing Your Child's Learning

Identify the areas in which your child needs improvement. Set goals, and phrase them in terms that are specific and achievable. For example, "My child will be able to tell me what his asthma triggers are" is a more specific, obtainable goal than "My child will understand asthma better."

Make a plan for you and your child to read through *Breathe Easy* systematically. Schedule time for reading sections of the book and practicing the exercises.

Place a chart on your refrigerator or on the wall of your child's room so that you can record each reading and practice session. Make room on the chart to write down your goals, and make a check mark each time you feel that your child has fulfilled one of the goals. For example, your child took medicine without being reminded or used the peak-flow meter correctly.

Give your child a reward for reading, practicing, and moving toward the goals you have set. The reward might be a fun activity you do together, something special to eat, or a small present. Try to use a different reward each time, because the same reward over and over can become less motivating. Remember that words can be rewarding, too, so praise your child when appropriate.

Be liberal with encouragement, praise, and rewards, especially at the beginning. Remember that practice makes perfect, so don't expect perfection right away. Try to overlook mistakes. What is important is effort, and you want to encourage your child to keep trying until he or she has mastered self-management. You can also help that process by learning the information and exercises in the book yourself so that you can answer your child's questions, demonstrate techniques, and give feedback and suggestions.

Let your child know right away when you see progress. That will encourage your child to keep working on controlling his or her asthma.

Resources

Organizations

You can find a wealth of information about asthma and allergies on the Internet. The following organizations have excellent Web sites, with information on the latest asthma research and treatments, how to find a doctor and a support group, educational and community awareness programs, pollen counts, and more. Many offer electronic newsletters that you can sign up to receive via e-mail.

Allergy and Asthma Network/Mothers of Asthmatics (AANMA)
www.aanma.org
2751 Prosperity Ave., Suite 150
Fairfax, VA 22030
(800) 878-4403

American Academy of Allergy, Asthma and Immunology
www.aaaai.org
611 E. Wells St.
Milwaukee, WI 53202
(414) 272-6071

American Lung Association (ALA)
www.lungusa.org
61 Broadway, 6th Floor
New York, NY 10006
(800) 386-3872

Asthma and Allergy Foundation of America (AAFA)
www.aafa.org
1233 20th St. NW, Suite 402
Washington, DC 20036
(800) 7-ASTHMA

Consortium on Children's Asthma Camps
www.asthmacamps.org
490 Concordia Ave.
St. Paul, MN 55103
(651) 227-8014

National Asthma Education and Prevention Program
National Heart, Lung, and Blood Institute Information
Center
http://www.nhlbi.nih.gov/about/naepp
P.O. Box 30105
Bethesda, MD 20824-0105
(301) 592-8573

U.S. Environmental Protection Agency
Indoor Environments Division
www.epa.gov/iaq
1200 Pennsylvania Ave. NW
Mail Code 6609J
Washington, DC 20460
(202) 564-9370

Web Sites for Kids

Kids can play online and learn at the same time. Here
are some Web sites that offer games, activities, stories,
tips, and fun quizzes for children and teenagers who want
to learn more about asthma and allergies.

Asthma Wizard
National Jewish Medical and Research Center Web site
www.nationaljewish.org/wizard/wizard.html

Explorers Club
Environmental Protection Agency Web site
www.epa.gov/kids

Fankids
Food Allergy & Anaphylaxis Network (FAAN)
www.fankids.org

Just For Kids
American Academy of Allergy, Asthma and Immunology
Web site
www.aaaai.org/patients/just4kids

Kids Corner
SchoolAsthmaAllergy.com
www.schoolasthma.com

Playtime
Allergy and Asthma Network/Mothers of Asthmatics
(AANMA) Web site
www.aanma.org/playtime

Pollen Index on the Internet
To get the pollen index for your area, visit these Web
sites and enter your Zip Code.

www.aaaai.org
www.pollen.com
www.schoolasthma.com